21 Tips and Tricks
To Enhance Your Game of Golf
And Play Like The Pros

Table of Contents

Introduction

Golf is much more than just swinging a club and hoping it makes it in. It's an art that can be mastered through constant and consistent tweaking of your technique. The art behind the swing is the magic behind winning or losing a game and it can be perfected through dedicated practice. However, one-upping your buddies at the course on a Saturday morning to see who buys the beer doesn't have to be hard work.

In fact, it's quite easy, and I've broken down some of the key techniques that you can use to do it. When you implement just a few of the tips and tricks from the following chapters into your weekly golf game, you'll start to see your score improve in no time (and will probably never have to buy the Saturday night beer again). So let's grab the putter and get to swingin'!

Chapter 1 – Tips to Improve Your Golf Swings

One of the most common questions that golfers have about the game is how to improve their golf swings. This is where this book will begin providing you with tips on how to improve your game. It's pretty undeniable that swinging golf clubs is at the heart of the action of this sport. So, without further ado, let us begin with the very first tip.

Tip #1 – Go Back to Basics

Golfers sometimes develop bad habits after swinging their golf clubs for quite some time. Some golfers watch how the pros take their shots and try their very best to mimic them. That may sound like a good idea at first, but that may not always work. What works for some players may not exactly work for you.

You know the basics of a golf swing. Your body should be able to move freely. The hips should be pushed back, the spine and your entire back should be angled toward the golf ball, and your knees should be slightly flexed. This posture is just like that of a bowler setting up for a throw – perfectly balanced without the need to adjust any weight.

Tip #2 – Body Power not Arm Strength

The basics of a good swing should teach you that you should use the power of your torso. That means you shouldn't rely on the strength of your arms. Doing so will also produce more consistent results with each swing.

Tip #3 – Details of a Backswing

Your backswing should be fundamental. It should come to you instinctively. As you move halfway back to your right side (if you're right handed, left side if you're left handed) you should be rotating your body clockwise (right handed). The shaft of your club should be intersecting your right shoulder when your forearms are parallel to the ground.

Once you're at the very top of your back swing with the club at the top, your left lat should be stretched. Your left arm shouldn't remain rigid, loosen it up a little bit. Your right ankle and hip should feel like they're ready to spring forward – that means they should feel a bit stretched.

You should begin your downswing with a lateral shift – but do it slightly. At this point your belt buckle should be pointing at the ball. When you finally swing the club, your arms (and the club) should be proverbially wrapped around your neck. Remember the basic forms. Sticking to the basics usually brings consistency.

Chapter 2 – Tips to Get Yourself Out of a Bunker

They didn't call them sand traps for nothing. Some golfers shiver at the thought of landing their balls in them. The good news is that there are ways to get out of the bunker in case you do find yourself stuck in one.

Tip #4 – Sand Wedge for Bunker Freedom

There are three things that you have to consider in order to get out of the bunker. They include consistent point of entry, proper technique, and correct setup. The "weapon of choice" when one is stuck in the sands is a sand wedge.

There are different sand wedge variants to choose from. When it comes to loft, they may range from 55 up to 58 degrees. Along with that, they may have some 8 to 12 degrees of bounce. Which sand wedge works for you will ultimately be up to you.

Tip #5 – Correct Set Up

In order to correctly set up your shot, you should first establish your target line. This is an imaginary line from the ball to the target. The heel of your left foot should be aligned with the ball. From there, create another imaginary line that is 10 degrees open from the target line and that will be the line that your feet make (well, particularly your toes).

Make sure that your weight is distributed equally on both feet. In order to add some loft on the ball, remember that the club's face should be a bit open. Make sure that the bottom of the club – particularly its back portion – should bounce off the sand. Note that the leading edge shouldn't dive right into the sand.

Tip #6 – Improve Your Point of Entry

One of the crucial things about bunker play is to make sure that you make a consistent point of entry every single time. This means that your wedge should enter the sand at the same spot for every forward swing you make. The correct point of entry is not to make the club hit the ball. Your club should slice into the sand a couple of inches behind the ball.

You can actually practice your swings while on the sands. Draw a straight line on the sand, which represents the area where the ball is. Draw another line two inches away from the first line. Now, it's time for you to swing away. Try to hit the line behind the first one each time you swing. Remember to use the force of your body when you swing. That way, you make consistent results as opposed to relying on the accuracy provided by your arms alone.

Chapter 3 – Chip Shot Tips

A chip shot, by definition, is a shot that is near the green. The ball pops up and then rolls forward towards the target. It can be done a few yards away from the green. Players usually prefer to do a chip shot using a wedge. However, you shouldn't be surprised to find other golfers hitting their chips with either a 7 iron or an 8 iron.

One of the most historic chip shots in golf history was made back in the 2005 Masters. It was done by no other than golf great Tiger Woods. It was in his hole-out at the Augusta National when he was on the 16th hole. You can find videos of this shot online using key phrases like "Tiger Woods Chip Masters Augusta" or some equivalent.

There is a difference between a chip shot and pitch shot and some people may mistake one for the other. Both shots are made from about the same distance, which may be the reason why others might think that they are one and the same. We'll discuss pitch shots in another section of this book. However, just to make it clear, the big difference between these two shots is that a chip shot mainly makes the ball pop up for a quick second or two and then roll, while a pitch will more likely make the ball go up in the air and roll for only a little bit.

Pitch shots have a comparably higher trajectory and are used to make the ball land closer to the pin. Simply put, if you want to make the ball roll on the ground then do a chip shot; but if you want to make the ball go up in the air and land closer to the pin, then do a pitch shot.

Tip #7 – The Golden Rule of Chip Shots – The 6-8-10 Rule

The rule of thumb when it comes to chip shots is to make sure that the ball doesn't fly up in the air too high. Keep it as low as possible. What you're trying to do is to make the ball gain some traction so that it can roll forward. The idea is more roll – less flight.

There are two factors that come into play when you try to chip a shot. The first one is the type of golf club you're using and the second one is the type of slope you've got in front of you. You should note that there is a ratio between the ground time and the air time of a ball and that ratio will change depending on the two aforementioned factors.

So, where does the 6-8-10 rule come in? The rule comes from estimates that have been made using a 6 iron, an 8 iron, and a 10 iron (also known as a pitching wedge). The assumption of course is that you're playing on a level green. The table below shows how much the ball will roll and how much the ball will fly up in the air towards the hole.

6 iron	Air time ¼ of the way/ground time ¾ of the way
8 iron	Air time 1/3 of the way/ground time 2/3 of the way
10 iron	Air time ½ of the way/ground time ½ of the way

So, what does this table mean? It means that on a level green, when you use a 10 iron to chip, then you should expect the ball to go up in the air up to half the distance towards the hole and then roll along the remaining half distance. If you chip using your 8 iron then you should expect the ball to stay in the air about a third of the way to the hole and then roll for the remaining distance. A six iron will make a ball pop up a quarter of the way and then roll along the remaining three quarters of distance.

Remember that the info on this table works for a level green. What do you do when you're on an uphill green? The answer is to go up on club. So, if you're using an 8 iron but you suddenly find yourself with an uphill then switch to a 6 iron. However, if you're playing downhill then switch to 10 iron.

Here's an additional tip: you should always try to land the ball at a distance of about three feet and then just let it roll the rest of the way on the putting surface.

Tip #8 – Golfer's Stance and the Proper Swing

To make a pitch shot you should begin with a golfer's stance. Put your weight on your front foot. You should also position your ball in between your two feet. Remember your hands should be slightly ahead of the golf ball. Given this position you're now ready to make your swing.

Remember that knowing which golf club to use is only half the battle. You should make sure that your left wrist, if you are right handed (or your right wrist, in case you're left handed) doesn't break down when you make your shot. Make sure to keep your arm straight when you swing and your left wrist (or right wrist if you're a leftie) should remain firm.

Remember that it will take a lot of practice before your get to make perfect chip shots. This means that you may have to skip some sessions at the driving range and spend more time at the chipping green.

Tip #9 – Shorten Your Backswing

This is our final tip on making chip shots – shorten your back swing. There are two common mistakes that people make when they are chipping. The first one is called the chunker, which is like a fat chip and the ball doesn't go anywhere. The other common chipping error is called a skull, a thin chip and it makes the ball shoot all the way across the green from one side to another.

Why do people make this mistake? The answer is simple, they are hitting up. They either hit the top of the ball with the sole or they strike the ground first. The solution of course is to shorten your backswing.

If you've been in the driving range too long, you should be well used to the idea of wrapping your club all around your neck. The thought of swinging back only hip level seems like a foreign idea. Most of the time, golfers who attempt this don't realize that they can make the ball go 25 to 30 yards forward. When you're attempting to make a chip shot, the average distance you're trying to cover is only 10 up to 15 yards. Again, you need to spend more time at the chipping green and less time at the driving range.

Chapter 4 – Pitch Shot Tips

The chip shot was highlighted in the previous chapter. Several tips on how to make better chip shots were also provided. Pitch shots were also described. There will be times when you just have to make pitch shots though conventional wisdom tells you that you should go for the chip in lieu of the pitch.

Nevertheless, knowing how to do both will greatly improve your game and eventually lower your scores. We'll look into pitch shots in this chapter. The following information explains the rudiments of making standard pitches.

What Makes a Pitch Shot

The primary differences between a pitch shot and a chip shot has been discussed in the previous chapter. Both these shots are made at a close distance from the green. The key to making pitches is distance. If chip shots are made from a distance of 25 to 30 yards away from the cup then a pitch shot is made from a distance that is a little further.

You can say that you will need to do a pitch shot when you're 30 to 100 yards away. Well, that is only a rough estimate. Some golfers are more skilled than others, thus some may consider a hundred yard distance as a pitch while others won't call it that. At any rate, you can say that a pitch shot is a close range shot that his a little further away from the green compared to a chip shot.

Tip #10 – Things to Keep in Mind

You should keep in mind a few factors when making a pitch shot. Just like in the case of the chip shot, the type of golf club you use will be a big factor. Some experts recommend using a sand wedge to make a pitch shot. Other than the golf club, you should also mind your set up, your grip, as well as your stance. All of these will play a role when you make this shot.

Tip #11 – The Proper Grip for a Pitch Shot

You don't actually have to change your grip when you make a pitch shot. Yes, use the same grip that you're comfortable with in the driving range. However, since you're trying to cover a shorter distance then here's what you need to do. The only thing different you're going to do is that you're going to position your hands a little lower on the golf club. This will help you hit the ball at a shorter distance.

The width of your stance should about shoulder length or shoulder width. You should balance your weight on both of your feet. Each foot should have an equal share of your body's total weight. You should also position the ball at the very center of your stance. This means that the ball should cut the distance between both feet. This means that you will strike the ball with a descending blow.

Tip #12 – The Right Swing

The swing you'll use will depend on the amount of distance you want to cover. Remember that the longer your swing the further the ball will go. Controlling the distance is the big secret to making a pitch shot. However, that doesn't mean that you should go on a full swing. You can call a pitch shot as a kind of mid-range shot. It's not a full swing, but it's longer than the swing you make for chip shot. You should vary the length of your swing depending on the distance you want the ball to go. Lengthen your backswing for longer pitch shots and shorten it for shorter distances.

Tip #13 – The 7, 8, and 9 O'clock Positions

The 7 o'clock, 8 o'clock and 9 o'clock positions refer to the position of your left arm (if you're right handed) or your right arm (if you're left handed) as you address the ball. You can imagine your arm as the arm of a clock pointing to 7, 8, and 9 o'clock. Make sure to cock your wrist when you swing. As you follow through with your shot, this will help you make a blow that is slightly downward. This will make backspin when you make a pitch shot (important detail).

Note how far and how high the ball goes up when you pitch your shots in the 7 o'clock position. Keep practicing this shot until you become more consistent. You know that you have it right when the ball travels about the same distance each and every time you make this shot. Remember the distance that can be covered with your 7 o'clock pitch shot.

Once you're done with the 7 o'clock shot then move your arm to the 8 o'clock position. Practice your swings at that arm position until you get more or less consistent results. After that, do the same thing when you put your arm in the 9 o'clock position. Note that when you're in the 9 o'clock position, your arm should be almost parallel to the ground. Next time you need to make a pitch shot, all you need to do is estimate the distance you have to cover and choose which arm position you're supposed to use to make that shot.

Tip #14 – Where to Place the Weight on Your Feet

When you address the ball, note that most of your weight should be on your front foot. That should be the standard when you're making a pitch shot. You should keep your body steady when you swing your club. Your weight should never shift to the back foot when you swing your pitches even when you're at the top of your backswing.

Tip # 15 – Pace of the Swing

Remember that the pace of the swing should remain consistent all throughout. Each and every time you swing your golf club, you should use the same pace. This will help you get more consistent results.

Tip #16 – Note Your Follow Through

The follow through is an important part of a pitch shot. Never intentionally stop your follow through when you make this shot. Doing that will make you come short with every shot you make. Your arms should be at the 3 o'clock position (more or less) when you make your follow through. Note that the follow through is pointing directly at your target. Your club and arms shouldn't wrap around your body.

Chapter 5 – When To Chip, Pitch, and Putt

Now that we've covered both the chip shot and the pitch shot, you now have the very workhorse of any short game on the green – well, short of putting; but we'll get there later. The next question is when do you do a chip shot and when do you do a pitch shot. Most experts advise that you should favor the chip shot over the pitch.

The reason behind this is that players don't have a lot of control when the ball goes up in the air. The wind may affect your shot especially if you weren't able to factor that into your estimates. The ball's movement becomes more predictable when it's rolling on the ground rather than when it's high up in the air.

That is why more players keep their best wedge close by when they are nearing the cup. Experts recommend that when a chip and run option is available then you should go for that instead of pitching a shot. Here are three important rules whenever you're at 50 or so yards (or anywhere close actually) to the green.

Tip #17 – 3 Important Rules to Live By

- **Rule #1 – Putt First**
  Whenever you see an opportunity to make the ball roll on the ground do it. This is especially true if the field is level and if it seems that the ball won't bounce.
- **Rule #2 – Chip Second**
  If you can't putt, then do a chip shot. If you can sink it in the hole then go for it. Otherwise just get the ball as close to the cup as you can.
- **Rule #3 – Pitch Third**
  If you can't putt and you can't chip, then you should pitch it. Pitch only when you have no other choice.

Tip #18 –Putt More Drive Less

Since the very first rule above says that you must putt as much as humanly possible then you must putt. That also means that if you have the slightest opportunity presents itself then you must putt. The question is how much time do you spend practicing your putts?

Most of the time, there are more people in driving range than in the green. Peter Morrice, renowned golf writer, once hinted that nearly 50% of the strokes you play on the field are done in the green. Unfortunately, many golfers spend less than 50% of their time practicing at the green.

So our first tip when it comes to putting is to spend more time practicing putts. Spend more time at the practice green. It will make you feel more comfortable during an actual game and you'll find that your scores have gone lower. If you have some extra cash and some space in your backyard, then you can construct your own practice green. It's going to save you some money in the long run and it will help you perfect your swing.

Tip #19 – Evaluate the Green

Our next tip is that you should also evaluate the green even while you're still in the fairway. Remember that the only perfect putting greens are the ones in the video games. No two greens are alike; and most of the time some of its parts are sloped at an angle.

The best time to study a green is when you're at a distance away from it. Some angles are obscured when the thing is right in front of you. The distance can give you a general view of the green's topography. Remember that almost all greens are typically sloped. Have you ever wondered why?

The answer is simple. The architects who designed them usually give them a slope so that the water drains quickly. You don't want the ground to remain soggy after some rain. Expect greens to be sloped. Find that slope from a distance and then make adjustments along the way. Keep studying the green as you get closer.

Another important feature of all greens that you should pay attention to is the fall line. Simply put, this is the contour of the green. If your ball lands on the right side of the fall line, expect it to break from right to left. If your ball lands on the opposite side then expect it to break from left to right.

You should concentrate on getting the proper form when you're putting. Some golfers try too hard to look like the pros when they're on the green that they fail to concentrate on getting the ball in. Well, looking like a pro doesn't mean you putt like a pro.

Keep things simple and use the posture that's most comfortable to you. Just make sure that you use your arms and shoulders to swing. Your wrists and your hands should be used to stabilize your putter. If that sounds pretty basic then that's basically what you should be doing. However, there are those who find that they do better at putting with at least some wrist action – well, if you're more comfortable with that then do it as long as it brings you the results you need.

Tip #20 – Fluidity of Strokes

Our next putting tip comes directly from Jack Nicklaus. He once commented that one of the most important things about putting is to make fluid strokes consistently. That might sound like someone asking you to act like a robot but that's not the point. Nicklaus explains further that in order to get that consistency in your motion, all you have to do is to loosen your grip.

Yes, a lot of golfers grip their putters too tight. Loosen your grip a bit and hold your putter firmly (but not too firm). Allow it to swing naturally with a little help from its own momentum carried by the putter's weight. You should grip it firm enough to still be able to control the face alignment and control its head path as well.

Putting short distances shouldn't make you sweat. You can see the hole, the ball, and you can already imagine the line that your ball must roll over so that it will go in. At that point, you can already estimate how much force you need for your backswing. It's a cinch. Well, putting short distances is one thing but putting from 20 feet away is a totally different animal.

Most of the time, putting from a distance will make a lot of golf players stack up on their scores. A slight error in your execution and your shot will be way off. That is why putting from a distance is enough to rattle the nerves even of very experienced golfers. The bottom line is that you can actually shave off a good deal of points by simply being able to make that long distance putt. So, how do you do it? Learn spot putting.

Keeping things as simple as possible, spot putting is visualizing an imaginary spot when you line up a shot. Aiming at and trying to hit something 20 feet away is difficult. No one is trying to refute that idea. However, somewhere along the path that your ball has to go through in order to make it to that hole are several spots. What you're doing is to simply connect the dots.

Spot putting is a visualization technique. Line up your shot. Try to imagine where your ball needs to roll onto in order to make it to the hole. Along that path is a spot that's about three feet or more in front of you. If your ball rolls along to that spot you are sure that your ball will go into the hole. What you need to do is to focus and aim for that spot, which is closer and easier to visualize than the actual target that is quite a distance away. Aim for that spot. Swing and make your ball go through it and you can be sure that if your ball makes it to that spot it will find its way into the hole.

The key to successful spot putting is correct visualization. A prerequisite to that is properly reading the green – rings a bell, doesn't it? You should have been reading the green earlier on and you should still be reading the green once you're right there.

As you read the green, you should also be able to visualize your putting line correctly. Now, to help you get a better estimate you should view the path of your ball all the way to the hole from at least two different perspectives. The first one is where you're looking at it, from somewhere behind the ball. The other way to look at the putting line is right over it.

When you have visualized the putting line walk over to it and look above it. There are times when your eyes will trick you when you look too far to the side, according to golf guru Mary Tiegreen. Visualize your putting line and stand over it and see if it is correct. Make any necessary adjustments if any.

Tip #21 – Don't celebrate too early

Okay, you may have made a successful putt. Well, alright, celebrate a bit but be quick about it. If you finally made a long distance putt then you can pat yourself in the back – but don't pop the champagne just yet. This next tip is important whether you made the hole or not.

Chances are there was something you could learn from the last shot you made. Sure you got the ball to the hole from 25 yards away with your trusty putter. Well, do you remember how you did it? Take the time to internalize everything that you did to make that shot. You should be able to retain most of it in your head and eventually commit it to memory, permanently. That's the way you move your game up a notch. You learn from both the mistakes and the failures.

If you failed to make the shot try to look back and recall what made you miss. Was there something that distracted you? Was your pre-visualization correct? Why did you make a mistake when you tried to translate it into actual execution? This is what Fred Shoemaker, another well-known golf guru, calls the debriefing session after a shot. Remember that it doesn't have to take that long. You just need a minute or two to get it done – after that you can celebrate.

Extra Tips – Putting Drills

Putting drills are a great way to practice. Note that different putting drills will help you with different aspects of the game. We'll go over a couple of distance control drills, which will be quite helpful for people who still need to learn to make short and long distance putts.

Putting Drill #1

Take three balls, place one 10 feet from the cup, another at 20 feet, and the last one at 30 feet. Try to sink the putt from each of these three distances. You won't always make it each time. However, make sure that in case you fail to sink it, the ball will remain within three feet from the hole.

And that's basically the idea behind this putting drill – you're establishing a plan A and a plan B. Plan A is to make the ball go into the hole no matter which distance you're hitting from. However, if you don't make it, you have a plan to fall back on. And that is in case you miss, you only need to make the putt with the shortest distance possible. This strategy is called lag putting.

Putting Drill #2

This second drill is also a lag putting drill and it's a lot easier to do. Grab five balls; try to putt them from a distance, somewhere around 20 to 30 feet from the cup. Each time you miss, walk over to the ball and try to putt it from a shorter distance.

Conclusion

Thank you again for reading this book!

I hope this book was able to help you to learn to perfect your golf game. I have been playing this game for over 20 years now, and I know that while technique is important, the biggest difference between the pros and amateurs is taking action.

So the next step is to get out onto the golf course and start using the practice instructions I taught you and watch your scores skyrocket!

Finally, if you enjoyed this book, then I'd like to ask you for a favor, would you be kind enough to leave a review for this book on Amazon? It'd be greatly appreciated!

Thank you and good luck!

Keep reading for a free preview of my next book:

*"Backpacking Light: The Ultimate Survival Guide
For Your First Backpacking Adventure"*

Chapter 2 – The many forms of backpacking

There are three forms of backpacking. Make sure you are knowledgeable in all three before you start any journey.

Backpacking cross-country or in your locality

Anyone who hasn't had any experience in backpacking should try this form of backpacking out at first. Backpacking cross-country or in your locality will uproot you from familiar surroundings without taking you too far from your comfort zone. This can be regarded as a test of your will power and drive to do backpacking before you take on bigger challenges.

Take a backpacking journey in your own locality for a day or two. This is a great way to rediscover the place you live in. After all, before you learn about the world shouldn't you know more about what's happening in your own surroundings?

If you're planning on doing the next two forms of backpacking, backpacking in this manner will help prepare your body for all the stresses it's going to go through in those journeys. You'll also be able to gauge your ability to handle stress and if the worst comes to the worst, you'll have access to health services or call someone to come pick you up for assistance.

Backpacking in the wilderness

Backpacking in the wilderness is one of the most popular ways to totally immerse your own self in nature. Unlike camping where you pitch your tent before going out to experience nature, backpacking in the wilderness means camping where night time reaches you or when you get tired.

Since you are going to be traversing rough terrain for the most part of your journey, a good pair of hiking boots is required and a good tent to sleep in or rest in should be high on your list of things to bring along.

Another way to backpack in the wilderness is to backpack with animals in tow. Backpacking with animals sometimes requires the use of horses or llamas but you can also bring along a small pack animal like a dog or a goat. Just remember that you shouldn't let the animals carry all of your stuff for you especially if it is clear that they cannot handle the entire load. Share the weight accordingly and you should have an excellent time traversing the area with a trusty pack animal along for the trip.

At the least, it's an excellent way for you to bond with your dog!

Backpacking around the world

Now backpacking around the world is the one most people are familiar with. This is also the best way to travel as it is a very economical and unorthodox approach to see places not all people have access to.

Instead of relying on what the brochure says on your travel package, you'll have a chance to experience the places you're visiting the way it is supposed to be experienced. The many unique surprises you'll find along the way through this manner of travel will give you more education than relying on your tour guide and the tour schedule.

So, if you want to have a real picture of the real world outside your window, backpacking is a good way to do that.

Chapter 3 – Basic gear you should have in your backpack

Backpacking today as compared to decades ago

With the advent of modern technology, backpacking nowadays isn't quite as hard as it was a few decades ago. And yet, its value in terms of character development and appreciation for the world around us has not diminished.

Backpacks have also become lighter and more ergonomic adding to better comfort and style. Nowadays there is no need to bring a lot of things that was deemed essential before. Things like maps, books, writing materials, cameras, compasses are a thing of the past. Nowadays all of these items can be found as features on the latest smart phones.

Items that serve many functions have essentially trimmed the weight the backpacker has to carry in order to survive in the wilderness or in another country.

These changes should be embraced and used to your advantage.

By capitalizing on modern technology's improvements you can do away with bulky items and make room for other stuff that you might need on your journey. A multi-purpose tool saves space and does not add too much weight to your pack. In fact, it might even save you from carrying too much weight as a multi-purpose tool is equivalent to more than 2 items you might need to carry. For example, a Swiss Army knife has a couple of screwdrivers, a file, a can opener, a spoon, a fork, a small saw, a corkscrew and of course, a knife included in its small package. Think of all the weight and space you've just saved because of that!

If you're interested in checking out the rest of this book, visit the link below!

http://www.books4everyone.com/backpacking

Printed in Great Britain
by Amazon.co.uk, Ltd.,
Marston Gate.